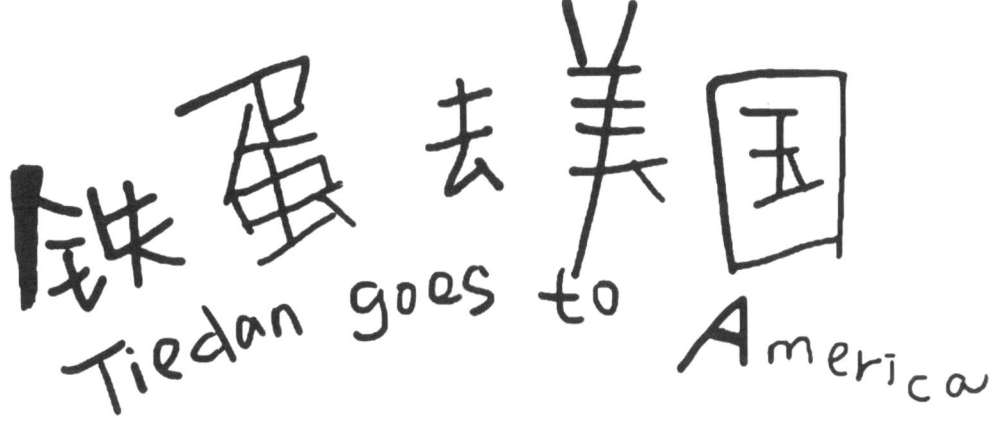

许丽涛
Brian J.Walthers 著

钟书国际文化出版社
BOOKLOVER INTERNATIONAL CULTURE PRESS,
AN IMPRINT OF METRO FIFTH AVENUE PRESS,LLC

TieDan goes to America © 2014 by Xu LiTao and Brian J. Walthers . Allrights reserved. Published in the United States of America. No part of thisbook may be used or reproduced in any manner whatsoever without written permission except in the case of brief quotations embodied in critical articles and reviews. For information, address Booklover International Culture Press, 551 Fifth Avenue, New York, NY10017.

本书的所有版权受到保护，未经出版者书面许可，任何人不得以任何方式和方法抄袭本书任何部分，违者须承担全部民事责任及刑事责任。

TieDan goes to America
铁蛋去美国

Author	Xu LiTao Brian J. Walthers
Editor	Zhang Qian
Design	Shirley
Publisher	Booklover International Culture Press
出版社	钟书国际文化出版社
Address	551 Fifth Avenue, New York, NY10017.
通讯地址	美国纽约第五大道551号，邮编10017
Acquisition	Beijing Booklover media CO., LTD.
Address	Dachen Road, Feng Tai Dist. Beijing, China.
策划组稿	众书网
	http://www.zbook.com
地　　址	北京市丰台区大成路6号大成时代中心2788室
邮　　编	100141
电　　话	010-88177119
电　　邮	Service@zbook.com
	2014年12月第1版　　2014年12月第1次印刷
开　　本	889mm×1194mm 1/16 印张：10.875 字数：33千字
ISBN	978-1-6260-9149-8
Price	$35.00

作者简介

许丽涛，19岁东渡日本，日本大阪大学经济系硕士，成绩优异，获文部省全额奖学金。曾在两家日本上市公司投资部门工作，精通日语、英语等多国语言及文化。通过在国外的学习生活经历，作者掌握了快速学习外语的方法——沉浸式语言学习法。

请关注新阶教育（微信号 xjeducation），里面有多语言学习的信息。

I'd like to take a moment to extend my greatest appreciation and admiration to you and your efforts in learning English (or Chinese). Being a language learner myself, I know very well the difficulties students experience at learning a second or third language. My own journey began back in high school where I took an interest in Japanese languages. I persevered and with hard work and determination I was able to obtain a Monbusho scholarship and eventually earning my Master degree in Economics from Osaka University. Achievements and setbacks are all part of the learning process and I hope to instill upon you some helpful advice that I was able to acquire from the many obstacles I was able to overcome. This book "Tiedan goes to America" is just a small element of my cultural knowledge and experiences of living abroad. It is with high hopes and humble gratitude that I and my friends put together these experiences of a small boy travelling for the first time in a new and wonderful country. So, put your best foot forward and make the most out of every page.

Warmest regards
Litao Xu

Brian J. Walthers,美国人,43岁,酷爱阅读,旅游。2005年来到中国上海,随后到贵州,河南,江苏等中国各地旅行并讲授英语。欢迎大家通过《铁蛋去美国》的体验经历来学习英语口语,这本书里的故事一定会丰富你的词汇,对你有所帮助,《铁蛋去美国》将给你带来欢乐,成为你学习英语的好帮手。

Hello and welcome to my personal introduction and greeting. First of all let me begin by saying that I am pleased and excited that you have chosen to become part of the English speaking community.

I came to China back in 2005 beginning my journey in Shanghai and continuing the adventure to the areas of Guizhou and Henan and Jiangsu. I am 43 years young and I believe that reading is one of life's great joys. Tiedan's journey and lessons on spoken English can enrich your own process of learning and communicating in English. Tiedan Goes to America can become one of your most treasured books and fill your days with happiness.

目录 Contents

前 言 / 1

铁蛋去美国 / 02

1. 铁蛋是谁 / 03
2. 铁蛋的日记 / 04
3. 铁蛋回给珍妮的邮件 / 07
4. 铁蛋给珍妮的另外一封邮件 / 09
5. 在机场 / 11
6. 在飞机上 / 14
7. 美国的历史 / 17
8. 在入境检查 / 18
9. 在海关 / 19
10. 在机场 / 20
11. 从机场到家 / 23
12. 到家了 / 25
13. 晚餐—礼仪 / 28
14. 晚餐—食物 / 30
15. 分礼物 / 33
16. 晚安 / 36
17. 早晨 / 38
18. 早餐 / 40
19. 谈论游乐园 / 43
20. 谈论游泳 / 45
21. 在路上 / 47
22. 关于学校 / 50

23. 到达游乐园 / 52
24. 排队等待 / 54
25. 坐上过山车 / 57
26. 哈哈屋 / 59
27. 休息 / 61
28. 买饮料 1 / 63
29. 买饮料 2 / 65
30. 采访 / 68
31. 讲演 / 70
32. 猜谜 / 72
33. 好消息 / 74
34. 午餐 / 76
35. 谈论中国 / 78
36. 关于沙滩 / 79
37. 学游泳 1 / 81
38. 学游泳 2 / 83
39. 在动物园 / 85
40. 骑骆驼 / 87
41. 喂羊 / 89
42. 家庭聚会 / 90
43. 参观美国小学 / 92
44. 暑假作业 / 94
45. 铁蛋爸爸妈妈写给
    珍妮爸爸妈妈的邮件 / 96
46. 珍妮妈妈写给
    铁蛋爸爸妈妈的邮件 / 98

目 录
Contents

Preface / 101

Tiedan goes to America / 106

1. Who is Tiedan / 107
2. Tiedan's diary / 108
3. An email / 110
from Tiedan to Jenny / 110
4. Another email / 111
from Tiedan to Jenny / 111
5. At the airport / 113
6. On the airplane / 115
7. America's history / 116
8. At immigration / 117
9. At customs / 118
10. At the airport / 119
11. Go home / 121
12. At home / 122
13. Dinner time1--manners / 124
14. Dinner time2—foods / 125
15. Presents / 127
16. Good night / 129
17. Morning / 130
18. Breakfast / 131
19. Talking about
Amusement park / 133
20. Talking about swim / 134
21. On the way / 135

22. Talking about school / 137
23. Arrived / 138
24. Wait in line / 139
25. Ride on roller coaster / 141
26. Fun house / 143
27. Take a break / 144
28. Buy drinks 1 / 145
29. Buy drinks 2 / 146
30. Interview / 148
31. Speech / 150
32. Quizes / 151
33. Happy news / 152
34. Lunch / 153
35. Talking about China / 154
36. At the beach / 155
37. Learn to swim 1 / 156
38. Learn to swim 2 / 157
39. At the Zoo / 158
40. Ride a camel / 159
41. Feed goats / 160
42. Homeparty / 161
43. Visit American school / 162
44. Summer Homework / 163
45. An email
from Tiedan's parents / 164
46. An email to
Tiedan's father and mother / 165

Tiedan goes to America

序 言

　　不要等到小学三年级（8岁）才开始学第一外语，高中或大学（16–18岁）开始学第二外语，那简直是时间和金钱上的浪费。只要你花一些时间，沉浸在铁蛋去美国的令人兴奋的旅行冒险之中，沿着铁蛋的脚步一步一个脚印地前进，你就能得到快乐学习外语的回报。儿童时期是学习外语的黄金时期。

　　《铁蛋去美国》以铁蛋为主人公，描写铁蛋去美国拜访寄宿家庭的故事，介绍美国人的生活环境、娱乐休闲等方面的信息，内容生动有趣、对话诙谐幽默。通过情景对话的形式，可以避免普通教材的简单枯燥。书中的对话内容全部使用常用、简单的初学者需要掌握的词汇。这套教材可以培养儿童对美国及英语的兴趣，提高英语听力和口语能力，是一本原汁原味地介绍美国风土人情的教材。

　　我们的中文版可以让初学者认识到多个汉字，同时掌握基础对话和口语表达。我们可以一边学习英语，一边提高汉语能力。在学习英语的同时提高汉语的能力。本书尝试使用多种语言同时教学的方法，力求在不放松学习一种语言的同时掌握多种语言。《铁蛋去美国》可以帮助您和孩子轻松快乐地学习外语。

丽涛 Litao

无锡外国语学校小学部周校长的推荐信

《铁蛋在美国》是一本很有意思的书,讲了铁蛋在美国寄宿的经历,读来如临其境。

《铁蛋在美国》给我的第一印象是真实记录了铁蛋的体验。从去美国前的相关准备,发邮件,乘飞机,过海关,到回国前与寄宿家人恋恋不舍的分别;从在飞机上不小心碰倒了杯子,将果汁洒在裤子上,铁蛋很尴尬紧张的细节描写,到自己与营业员交流,购买饮料;从参观学校,游玩乐园,逛店购物,到家庭聚会,都是铁蛋在美国寄宿体验的真实记录。其次是生动有趣。偌大无比的游乐场,刺激的过山车,变化多端的哈哈屋,是那么的妙趣横生。三是处处洋溢着快乐。"玩得开心",是书中出现最多的。铁蛋来到美国后,受到寄宿家庭的热情招待,他给新家的人分礼物,给他们带去快乐,使铁蛋兴奋得难以入睡;玩游乐园、学游泳、骑骆驼,玩得也很是开心;接受采访、讲演、猜谜,为史密斯家人赢得到中国旅游的机会,更是令大家欣喜不已。四是相互传递着文化。在美国寄宿期间,铁蛋了解了纽约的绰号是"大苹果";美国是1776年建立的;一美元钞票上的头像是美国第一任总统乔治·华盛顿。铁蛋在感受到美国人吃晚饭时祷告上帝的礼仪文化和一日三餐怎么吃的餐饮文化以及"在美国学校没有标准答案,你没有必要遵循老师的意见,但是你必须给出能解释得通的理由"的学校文化的同时,铁蛋也向美国人介绍了中国的北京、中国的哈哈镜、烟花、西瓜、草帽……铁蛋成了美国寄宿家庭了解中国的窗口。

铁蛋在美国欣赏了异土风情,体验了异国生活,了解了异质文化,结交了"异乡"朋友,是一次刻骨铭心的人生经历。

无锡外国语学校周校长

Tiedan goes to America

铁蛋去美国

主要人物：

铁蛋 —— 一个中国男孩

珍妮 —— 一个美国女孩

吴先生 —— 铁蛋的爸爸

许女士 —— 铁蛋的妈妈

钱老师 —— 铁蛋的英语老师

瑞瑞 —— 铁蛋的新朋友

史密斯先生 / 杰克逊 —— 珍妮的爸爸

史密斯太太 / 爱丽丝 —— 珍妮的妈妈

泰德 —— 珍妮的哥哥

爱德华 —— 珍妮的弟弟

索菲亚 —— 珍妮的姐姐

贝拉 —— 珍妮的妹妹

1. 铁蛋是谁

铁蛋是一个可爱而淘气的男孩,他今年12岁,是国际小学6年级的学生,他特别喜欢参加幸福家庭俱乐部的活动(幸福家庭俱乐部是一个多语言多文化的儿童活动俱乐部)。铁蛋会讲点英语,他对什么事都充满好奇心。他喜欢海外旅游。今年暑假铁蛋要到美国家庭寄宿。我们跟他一起去看看吧。

2. 铁蛋的日记

日期：6月22日 星期一

天气：晴朗

夏天来了，天气变得越来越热。我希望快点去美国，因为我想学习英语和美国文化。这是我去海外寄宿之前需要做准备工作的清单：

① 收集与美国相关的书籍和小册子

② 学习基础英语会话

③ 申请护照

④ 致函寄宿家庭

⑤ 制定时间表：计划天数，预算，去哪儿和目的

Tiedan goes to America

⑥ 在旅行社预订航班和办理签证

⑦ 兑换美元

⑧ 购买海外保险

⑨ 准备常用药

⑩ 买礼物给寄宿家庭

⑪ 收拾行李

我的签证没被批准，我不知道选择哪家旅行社为好，我最好请妈妈帮忙。

3. 铁蛋回给珍妮的邮件

亲爱的珍妮：

你好！珍妮。

我叫铁蛋，我真高兴能认识你。我和你一样12岁。邮件附件里有我的照片。我住在北京的东部，是小学六年级的学生。在学校里我参加了跆拳道学习班，我喜欢下围棋和画画，还特别喜欢幸福家庭俱乐部。

我的家庭成员有姥姥，姥爷，爸爸，妈妈和我。我的姥姥，姥爷已经70多岁了，但是他们身体很健康。我爸爸是软件公司的工程师，我妈妈是老师。我的舅舅也

住在北京,他每个周末都来看我。他是大学老师。我已经等不及夏天了,一定会很有意思,我想去美国快点和你见面。

你的朋友:铁蛋

4. 铁蛋给珍妮的另外一封邮件

亲爱的珍妮：

嗨，珍妮。

非常高兴收到你的邮件和照片。我很高兴认识你。非常感谢你邀请我到你那里寄宿。这是我第一次出国。我很兴奋、激动。

我将于7月8日下午4时抵达纽约机场。能不能请你的妈妈到机场接机？我会乘坐中国国际航空公司CA982的飞机。我盼望着早日见到你。

你的铁蛋

5. 在机场

铁蛋到柜台办理登机手续，他向工作人员出示了自己的护照。

铁蛋说：我想办理登机手续。

机场工作人员说：您想要靠窗的座位还是靠过道的座位？

铁蛋说：我想要靠过道的座位。

机场工作人员说：这是登机卡。请在十一点前于D号门登机。

铁蛋说：谢谢！

铁蛋在机场里闲逛，有这么多漂亮的品牌商店。

铁蛋想：这里的东西是一流的，但是

价格实在太高了，我买不起。我最好尽快离开这里。

Tiedan goes to America

6. 在飞机上

机内播放：请乘客系好安全带，飞机将在十分钟内起飞。

空姐问：你想喝点什么？

铁蛋回答：苹果汁。

空姐问：你想吃肉（盒饭）或吃鱼（盒饭）？

铁蛋回答：我想吃鱼（盒饭）。

铁蛋自言自语道：哦，这么多食物！有面包和黄油、鱼和蔬菜沙拉和苹果块。啊，味道非常好。

铁蛋说：我可以再喝一杯苹果汁吗？

空姐说：可以，给你。

铁蛋想：飞机上喝饮料免费续杯。

太好了。

铁蛋是太激动了,他不小心碰到了杯子,果汁洒在他的裤子上。他显得尴尬和紧张。

铁蛋:我该怎么办?

乘务员:没关系。我会用抹布帮你擦干净。

铁蛋:我很感谢你的帮助。

乘务员:不客气。这是我的工作。

7. 美国的历史

铁蛋读了一本书。书上说，"美国是一个联邦共和国，有50个州。华盛顿是其首都。联合国总部设在纽约。自从哥伦布发现美洲大陆之前，美洲印第安人是这片土地的原住民。后来来自欧洲各地的大量欧洲移民来到这里寻找美国梦。1776年，美国在对英国的战争胜利后美国获得了独立，美利坚合众国的历史从那一刻开始了新的一页。"

8. 在入境检查

海关官员说：我可以看一下你的护照吗？

铁蛋递给官员护照。

海关官员问：你来访的目的是什么？

铁蛋回答：我来参加一个寄宿家庭活动。

海关官员问：你打算呆多久？

铁蛋回答：一个月。

海关官员问：你带了多少现金？

铁蛋回答：我有500美元。

海关官员在铁蛋的护照上盖了一个章，铁蛋通过了入境检查。

 9. 在海关

海关官员问：你有什么东西要申报的吗？

铁蛋回答：不，我没有要申报的东西"。

海关官员要求铁蛋打开他的手提箱。

海关官员问：那是什么？

铁蛋回答：这是我的私人物品，这些是给寄宿家庭买的礼物。

海关人员让铁蛋合上手提箱走了。

10. 在机场

铁蛋想：刚开始我该说什么好呢？我想我应该说"How do you do?"，因为这是我们第一次见面。我有史密斯太太的手机号码。如果我迷路了，我会打电话给她。

哦，看看这些美国人，他们都是白皮肤，棕色的头发和蓝色的眼睛。他们带的行李也比我的重得多。

铁蛋看到有人举的牌子上写着他的名字，铁蛋走近看看。

史密斯太太高兴地说：你就是铁蛋。很高兴见到你。

铁蛋说：对不起，能不能请您慢慢地说？

Tiedan goes to America

史密斯太太慢慢地说：喔，对不起。你是铁蛋？"

铁蛋说：是的，你一定是史密斯太太。

史密斯太太说：是的。你真是和你的照片一模一样。我们很高兴见到你。你旅途愉快吗？

铁蛋回答：一路上还算顺利，不过坐14小时的飞机让我很疲劳，我得倒时差。不管怎么说，我很高兴来到这里。

史密斯太太说：你会感觉好起来的。咱们现在就走吧。

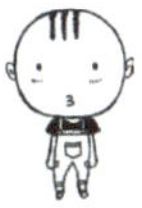

11. 从机场到家

shǐ mì sī tài tai hé tiě dàn yī qǐ shàng le yí liàng dà
史密斯太太和铁蛋一起上了一辆大
qì chē
汽车。

shǐ mì sī tài tai wèn tiě dàn tiě dàn dǔ zi è le
史密斯太太问铁蛋：铁蛋，肚子饿了
ba
吧？

tiě dàn huí dá ng yǒu diǎn xiè xie nín lái jiē wǒ
铁蛋回答：嗯，有点。谢谢您来接我，
shǐ mì sī tài tai
史密斯太太。

shǐ mì sī tài tai shuō bié jiè yì nǐ jiào wǒ ài lì sī
史密斯太太说：别介意。你叫我爱丽丝
jiù xíng
就行。

tiě dàn huí dá hǎo de ài lì sī
铁蛋回答：好的，爱丽丝。

tiě dàn zì yán zì yǔ dào wā hái shi měi guó
铁蛋自言自语道：哇！还是美国
ya shén me dōu dà nà me dà de měi guó qì chē yuán
呀，什么都大，那么大的美国汽车。原
lái zài měi guó hé zài zhōng guó yí yàng qì chē yě shì yòu
来在美国和在中国一样，汽车也是右
cè tōng xíng
侧通行。

shǐ mì sī tài tai wèn tiě dàn nǐ zhī bù zhī dào niǔ
史密斯太太问：铁蛋，你知不知道纽

约的别名?

铁蛋回答:我不知道。

史密斯太太说:纽约的别名是大苹果,因为他很有魅力所以每个人都想咬一口。

铁蛋说:真的?

铁蛋说:呵!麦当劳,肯德基,巨无霸在打对折。中国也有呀。

12. 到家了

史密斯太太说：到家了，铁蛋下车吧

铁蛋大喜：到了！好大的房子呀。后面还有个大花园。

史密斯太太说：铁蛋，今年夏天这就是你的新家了。

铁蛋说：是吗？真好，简直不能相信。

珍妮自告奋勇地说：欢迎来我们家。我带你去转转。楼上有4个卧室，楼下有客厅，厨房，餐厅。这是你的房间。

铁蛋高兴地说：很漂亮！这有一个黄色的衣柜，红色的橱柜，黄色的桌子，粉红色的书架和一张蓝色的床。书

架上有很多书和两个玩具。我可以从窗子里面看到外面的花和树木。这个房间是属于我的吗？

珍妮说：是的，橱柜的下层请你用吧。你可以把夹克挂到衣柜里，把其他衣服放在橱柜里。要洗的东西放在这个篮子里。我们一般一周洗两次衣服。如果你要打扫房间，请用这个吸尘器。

铁蛋突然问珍妮：珍妮，卫生间在哪？

珍妮说：你是指洗手间？跟我来，这就是洗手间。

Tiedan goes to America

13. 晚餐—礼仪

铁蛋问:你们通常什么时候吃晚饭?

史密斯太太说:我们七点左右吃。马上就好。铁蛋赶紧洗手吃饭。

史密斯太太说:铁蛋,请坐在杰克逊和泰德中间。

史密斯先生说:过来,坐在我的旁边。

铁蛋说:好吧。

祷告后,他们开始吃饭。铁蛋看到有许多食物放在一张长桌子上。中间有一个大盘鸡。铁蛋面前,有一个盘子、一把刀、一个勺子、一个叉子。虽然

Tiedan goes to America

没有筷子，但铁蛋不着急。铁蛋用右手拿刀、左手拿叉。这是西餐的礼仪。铁蛋也知道吃饭的时候嘴里有东西是不能说话的。

14. 晚餐—食物

史密斯太太拿起一碗沙拉从中捡了一些水果，然后把它传递给泰德。

史密斯太太说：铁蛋，我总是这样吃饭，每个人轮流捡一些菜到自己碗里。你尽管挑你喜欢的东西吃吧。

铁蛋说：好，谢谢！

泰德说：妈妈，给我盐。

史密斯太太说：好，给你。

史密斯太太说：索菲亚，要不要尝尝这些肉？

索菲亚说：不，我不要。我正在减肥。

史密斯太太说：好吃吗？铁蛋。

Tiedan goes to America

铁蛋说：好吃极了。

史密斯太太说：好哇，多吃点。

铁蛋说：不用了，谢谢，我已经吃不下了。

史密斯太太说：在中国你们晚餐都吃什么？

铁蛋回答：我们通常吃鱼，肉，蔬菜，包子和粥。这是典型的中国菜。

史密斯太太点头：喔。

铁蛋去美国

Tiedan goes to America

15. 分礼物

晚饭后，正好大家都在这里，铁蛋站起来大声说：大家注意了，这是我从中国带来的礼物。

铁蛋说：这是给杰克逊的，是我画的。

史密斯先生说：很好，让我看看。我会挂在冰箱上面的。

铁蛋说：很好。

铁蛋说：这是给你的，珍妮。

珍妮说：我可以打开吗？哈！是一件跟你身上穿的一模一样的T恤衫。

铁蛋说：是的，我妈妈给我买了一件新T恤衫。我很喜欢，所以我也买了一件

送给你。你喜欢吗?

珍妮说:我非常喜欢。谢谢你送我这么可爱的礼物,铁蛋。

铁蛋说:不用谢,我很高兴你能喜欢它。

史密斯太太说:好了好了。已经晚了,大家都去睡觉吧。

大家都说:好的,妈妈。谢谢你,铁蛋!

Tiedan goes to America

16. 晚安

铁蛋洗了脸,刷完牙,上床睡觉。但他因为太兴奋而难以入睡。

铁蛋想:这床真软真舒服。夜晚真是安静而漫长。虽然我连how do you do 也忘记说了,我讲的英文他们能听懂。有时我听到跟故事里面一模一样的句子,这真是太不可思议了。虽然我不能完全听懂他们在说什么,但我能猜出来大概意思。我把一些玉米掉在地上,但史密斯太太也没生气。他们对我可真好啊!

这次活动对我来说真是个很好的锻炼机会。万事开头难。我一定会适应

Tiedan goes to America

的。熟能生巧，明天我一定争取说更多的英语。

17. 早晨

在一个炎热的夏天早上,树上的蝉在唱着歌。铁蛋被他的外国朋友珍妮叫醒。

珍妮:(唤醒沉睡的家伙)……该起床了。用微笑迎接每一天。

铁蛋:(很困的)别管我,我困了。

珍妮:看,铁蛋。不要赖床,你最好马上起来。

铁蛋:啊!你每天早上都这么愉快?顺便问一下,几点了?

珍妮:(在床上跳)快点!!!起床了!已经7点了。今天是一个特别的日子。

Tiedan goes to America

铁蛋：（有点清醒）真的，今天是什么特别的日子？

珍妮：（站在门口）如果你能穿好衣服下楼来，你会知道的！

铁蛋飞快地穿上裤子，T恤衫和袜子。洗完脸后，他走下台阶。

18. 早餐

史密斯太太说：我们早餐一般吃麦片粥，我想你大概不喜欢，我们早饭吃法国土司好吗？

铁蛋回答：真棒。

当铁蛋看到法国吐司，他有点吃惊：我原来认为是法国长面包。您是怎么做的？

史密斯太太解释说：这很容易。你把面包切成片。然后你再把一个鸡蛋和牛奶混合在一起。把面包两面都蘸上鸡蛋和牛奶的混合物。煎锅里烧热油或黄油，放入面包煎这一面。两三秒后，翻转面包再煎另一面。最后，法国吐司就做好了。你可以沾枫叶糖浆吃。

铁蛋：好！

铁蛋去美国

19. 谈论游乐园

早餐过后，大家准备出发。

铁蛋对史密斯先生说：杰克逊，发生了什么，每个人都很兴奋！

史密斯先生回答：这是应该的，今天我们要去游乐园和水上公园了。

铁蛋：嗯，什么是游乐园？

索菲亚：你听说过一个叫"迪斯尼"的地方或一个著名的老鼠叫"米奇"？

铁蛋：当然。每个人都有听说过米奇。我喜欢他们的电影和动画片。

索菲亚：嗯，如果你知道迪斯尼乐园，那游乐园就像迪斯尼乐园，可能更小点。水上公园就象在沙滩上玩一天。

铁蛋:哇!!!听起来很有趣。你们以前去过吗?

索菲亚:是的。我们去过许多次了。这是我们在炎热的夏天里最喜欢去的一个地方。

20. 谈论游泳

tài dé hēi tiě dàn nǐ chōngguòlàng ma
泰德：嘿，铁蛋，你冲过浪吗？

tiě dàn wǒ yǒu guò shàng wǎng chōng làng nǐ zhǐ de
铁蛋：我有过上网冲浪，你指的

shì shàngwǎng ma
是上网吗？

tài dé wēi xiào zhe yòng shǒu zuò bō làng de dòng
泰德：（微笑着用手做波浪的动

zuò bù wǒ de yì si shì zài shuǐshangchōnglàng
作）不，我的意思是，在水上冲浪。

tiě dàn é zài shuǐ shang chōng làng méi yǒu wǒ
铁蛋：哦，在水上冲浪。没有，我

bú tài huì yóuyǒng
不太会游泳。

tài dé ng wǒ men xiǎng ràng nǐ zài zuì duǎn shí jiān
泰德：嗯，我们想让你在最短时间

xué huì yóu yǒng nǐ zuì hǎo qù wèn wèn mā ma zěn me yóu yǒng
学会游泳。你最好去问问妈妈怎么游泳，

tā shì jiā li yóuyǒng zuì bàng de
她是家里游泳最棒的。

tiě dàn hēi mā ma wǒ men qù shuǐ shang gōng
铁蛋：嘿！妈妈，我们去水上公

yuán zhī qián nǐ néng jiāo wǒ yóuyǒng ma
园之前，你能教我游泳吗？

shǐ mì sī tài tai yóu yǒng shì yí xiàng hěn hǎo de yùn
史密斯太太：游泳是一项很好的运

动，但它对初学者来说并不容易。首先，你必须要有足够的勇气，把你的头和身体伸到水里。然后，在水下屏住你的呼吸。

第三，放松地浮在水面。第四，学会在水里呼吸。最关键的是，我可以告诉你所有的游泳的技巧，但你只有在水中才能真正学会游泳。当我们到了那儿，我会帮助你的。

铁蛋（心想）：我希望我能学会游泳，这样，我在中国的朋友会为我感到高兴的。

Tiedan goes to America

21. 在路上

每个人都上了汽车，汽车朝游乐园行驶着。车上每个人都在欣赏沿途的风景。爱德华突然开始唱自己喜欢的歌，"老麦当劳有一个农场 Old McDonald had a farm"。铁蛋也跟着快乐地唱起来，因为这一首歌他在幸福家庭俱乐部里学过。

铁蛋：我知道这首歌，它讲的是农夫拥有一个农场，这个农场有很多动物。在歌里有提到这些动物的名字和模仿它们的声音……对吗？

爱德华：是的，铁蛋。你可以开始领唱了。

于是,他们一起大声唱:老麦当劳有一个农场,E, I E, I, O,在这个农场里有一只鸭子,E, I E, I, O,这里"嘎嘎"那里"嘎嘎",到处"嘎嘎"……,E, I E, I, O。

爱德华:铁蛋,真的。你唱得很好。你模仿的声音也很像。

铁蛋:谢谢你,爱德华。这首歌我在幸福家庭俱乐部学过。我们几乎每次聚会都会唱它。

Tiedan goes to America

22. 关于学校

铁蛋：我也知道一首歌就叫"车轮 Wheels on the bus"，你知道吗？

贝拉：我知道。那是我最爱的歌曲之一。我上学的时候我们经常唱那首歌。

铁蛋：我从没坐过校车。我看过一个美国校车的照片。它是黄色的，而且很大。据说他比其他任何汽车都结实。

贝拉：铁蛋，你怎么去学校？你步行去上学还是爸爸开车送你？

铁蛋：我们家离学校很近，所以我通常跟妈妈走着上学。有时爸爸开车送我。

Tiedan goes to America

贝拉：你最喜欢哪一科？

铁蛋：英语是我最喜欢的科目。钱老师是我的英语老师。她的英语讲得很流利，她给我们讲许多英语故事，如三只小猪。我们都喜欢她讲的故事。

贝拉：很好。

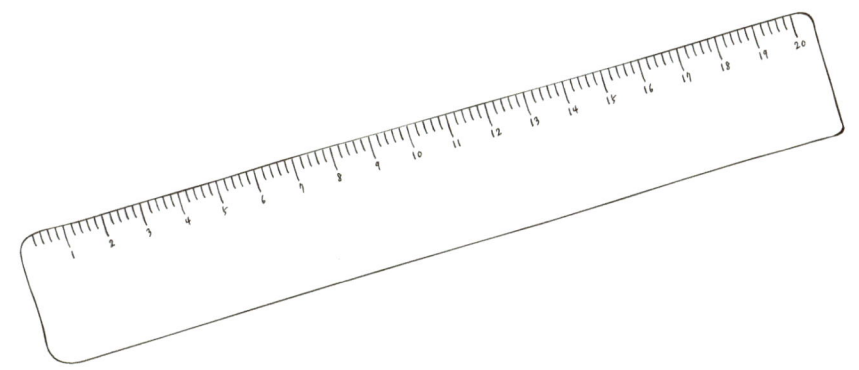

23. 到达游乐园

史密斯先生：大家好，我们到游乐园了。现在讲一些基本规则：

1. 把垃圾扔到垃圾桶里。

2. 不要单独行动。

3. 如果你迷路了，走到大门口，在那里等待。你们的妈妈或我将在那里。

4. 最重要的规则是……每个人要开心！！

大家都下了车，开始走向大门。

铁蛋：这真的是一个很有趣的地方！我很兴奋。

史密斯太太：铁蛋……你留在珍妮的

Tiedan goes to America

一个兄弟或姐妹身旁吧。这个地方很大,你很容易迷路。所以,要知道其他人在哪里,好吧?

铁蛋:是的,我会小心的。

珍妮:铁蛋,和我在一起,我们会很开心。我知道这里最好的游乐设施和最好吃的食物。

铁蛋:好的,听起来像对我很照顾。

24. 排队等待

每个人都进入公园,开始一段美好的时光。珍妮和铁蛋径直去坐过山车。他们在排一条很长的队伍。

珍妮:这是游乐园里最大的过山车,它的名字叫"野兽"。这全是木头做的,有3个大的山丘和一些很大的坡。你以前坐过过山车吗?

铁蛋:没有,没有这个大!我们北京有一个小游乐园,里面有过山车,摩天轮,海盗船和旋转木马。

珍妮:真的!我很喜欢摩天轮。你从那里可以看到整个游乐园。

铁蛋:这个队伍前进得很慢,我们得

Tiedan goes to America

花多少时间才能排到前面去?

珍妮:我不知道,但它值得等待。我希望你不会害怕。

铁蛋:哪有的事!越可怕,我就越喜欢。

Tiedan goes to America

25. 坐上过山车

两个人排队等候了一段时间,最后终于排到队伍的前面了。珍妮决定坐在列车的前面。

珍妮:这是最好的座位,铁蛋!来吧,坐下来,系上安全带。

铁蛋:哇!这肯定是一个很刺激的过山车。为什么称它为野兽?

珍妮:一会儿你就知道了!不要害怕。

铁蛋:好吧,让我们出发吧!!

这两个人像火箭一样在山上快速地扭曲旋转着。两个人都发出尖叫声和笑声。对铁蛋来说,这真是刺激而开心,他已经等不及要再坐一次了。

26. 哈哈屋

坐完过山车,珍妮和铁蛋决定去哈哈屋。

铁蛋:珍妮,我们现在去哪?

珍妮:一个被称为哈哈屋的地方。里面是一些镜子,让你看上去很怪。有些会使你看起来更高,更矮,更胖或更瘦。

铁蛋:哦,在中国我们也有类似的东西。我们叫它"哈哈镜"。

珍妮:听起来在中国有很多有趣的事。

铁蛋:当然,我们有很多有趣的事情。我最喜欢的是看烟花。

珍妮：烟花！！我爱看烟花，我们7月4日去公园看烟花。

铁蛋：在中国，你几乎每一天都可以看到烟花，过生日或什么节日，或其他的原因。

珍妮和铁蛋进入哈哈屋，从里面我们可以听到人们欢乐的笑声。后来他们出现在门口，两个人都在裂开嘴大笑。

27. 休息

珍妮：嗨，看那边，妈妈和爸爸！我以为他们去商店买纪念品了。

铁蛋：好啊！我渴了。我肯定能喝上饮料了。

珍妮（对史密斯先生和太太大喊）：妈妈，爸爸！

铁蛋：他们听到你了。他们正朝这边走来。

珍妮和铁蛋与史密斯先生和太太在公园中心旁边的喷泉边碰面。铁蛋很渴，他请史密斯先生给他买杯饮料。

铁蛋：史密斯先生……嗯……我的意

思是，杰克逊，我能喝点东西吗？

史密斯先生：当然了，铁蛋，你想喝什么？

铁蛋：我一直想试试柠檬汁。我在一次电视节目上看到它只要5美分。

史密斯先生：啊，你想尝尝柠檬汁。我想价格会超过5美分的。让我们去小卖部看个究竟。

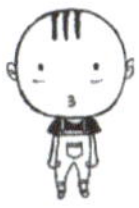

28. 买饮料 1

shǐ mì sī xiān sheng hé tiě dàn qù xiǎo mài bù, shǐ mì
史密斯先生和铁蛋去小卖部，史密
sī tài tai hé zhēn nī zài pèn quán páng xiū xi
斯太太和珍妮在喷泉旁休息。

zài xiǎo mài bù yǒu hěn duō kǒu kě de rén, dà jiā dōu
在小卖部有很多口渴的人，大家都
pái zhe cháng cháng de duì wu, děng dài lún dào tā mén diǎn yǐn
排着长长的队伍，等待轮到他们点饮
liào. tiě dàn kàn jian cài dān shàng yǒu hěn duō yǐn liào, nǎi
料。铁蛋看见菜单上有很多饮料，奶
chá, guǒ zhī, niú nǎi hé sū dǎ shuǐ, zuì hòu tā fā xiàn le
茶，果汁，牛奶和苏打水，最后他发现了
níng méng shuǐ
柠檬水。

tiě dàn: wā! yí fèn dà bēi níng méng shuǐ shì 5 měi
铁蛋：哇！一份大杯柠檬水是5美
yuán, tài guì le
元，太贵了。

shǐ mì sī xiān sheng: shì de, hěn guì. bú guò nǐ kě
史密斯先生：是的，很贵。不过你可
yǐ zì jǐ diǎn lái cháng cháng
以自己点来尝尝。

tiě dàn: shén me? yǔ mò shēng rén jiāo tán huì lìng wǒ jǐn
铁蛋：什么？与陌生人交谈会令我紧

张的，我不知道说什么好。

史密斯先生：我相信你能做到。只要用词简单，慢慢说就行。

铁蛋：好的，我会努力的！看我的。

Tiedan goes to America

29. 买饮料2

铁蛋走向柜台，咽了一口唾沫，他好不容易开口说话了。收银员站在柜台后面看着他，以极大的耐心听他说话。

铁蛋：对不起，我想要一杯饮料。

收银员：好的，你想喝什么？

铁蛋：我要份中柠檬水加很多冰块。

收银员：你想要新鲜柠檬吗？

铁蛋：什么？"新鲜"是什么意思？

收银员："新鲜"意味着……不老。

铁蛋：好的，我想要一些新鲜的柠檬在里面。

收银员：好吧……这杯饮料是3.50美元。

铁蛋：好的……这是一个5美元。能不能找给我零钱？

收银员：是的，当然……你的零钱是1.50美元。

铁蛋：谢谢。

收银员：祝你在游乐园里玩得开心。

Tiedan goes to America

30. 采访

铁蛋和史密斯先生回到珍妮和史密斯太太在的喷泉旁。美国ABC电台记者与摄影师来到铁蛋身旁。

记者：你好，我们正在制作一期电视旅游节目，能采访你吗？

铁蛋：是的，当然。我是从中国来的交流学生。

记者：好，你可以跟我们的观众分享一些你对美国的印象吗？我们会录像的。

铁蛋：好。让我试试。

记者：然后，我会问你一些简单的问

题。如果你回答正确，你会为你的寄宿家庭赢得往返中国旅游的机会。

31. 讲演

记者说：今天是美好的一天，我是美国ABC电台记者在游乐园。我们很高兴认识一个新朋友，他叫铁蛋，一个从中国来的小学生。他穿着一件蓝色的棉T恤。现在，铁蛋，请跟我们的观众分享你的一些有关美国的感想。

铁蛋说：这是我第一次来纽约。纽约是个大城市。一切都是美好的。我的寄宿家庭是对我太好了。我很高兴，我遇到的和跟我说话的每个人对我都很友好，我能交到许多新朋友。

Tiedan goes to America

今天我来到这个游乐园。我坐了一个过山车叫野兽。这个过山车很惊险刺激。我还会尝试更多的游乐设施。我相信我一定会玩得很开心。在接下来的几天里，我将参观博物馆，动物园还有美国小学校。这是一次非常好的人生体验，这些经历对我将来会很有帮助。感谢ABC电台的观众。谢谢大家！

32. 猜谜

记者：你的演讲很精彩，很好。接下来，让我给你出几个小题目，可能对你来说是个挑战。准备好了吗？

铁蛋：是的，我准备好了。

记者：第一个问题，纽约的绰号是什么？

铁蛋：大苹果（想到史密夫太太在接他回家的路上告诉他的）

记者：你很聪明。下一个问题，美国是什么时候建立的？

铁蛋：1776年（想到他在飞机上看到的那本书。）

记者：第三个问题是，谁的头像印在

Tiedan goes to America

1 美元钞票上?

铁蛋:乔治·华盛顿,美国第一任总统(想到那天珍妮告诉他的)。

记者:太好了。完全正确!祝贺你赢得了往返中国旅游的机会。恭喜恭喜!

铁蛋:我很幸运。谢谢!

33. 好消息

史密斯先生：哇！真是太棒了！我们什么时候出发？**记者**：这个奖励最棒的部分是可以选择。你可以选择在明年的任何时候出发。所有人！

铁蛋：哇！这意味着史密斯全家可以来中国看我的家人，这样你们就能看到我给你们介绍的那些好地方了。

珍妮：是的。这真是一个好消息……我都等不及要告诉其他人了。

全家外出寻找爱德华，贝拉，索菲亚，泰德，想把这个好消息告诉他们。最后，找到了他们。珍妮是第一个告诉他们这个好消息的人,他们都高兴地计划怎样去中国。

34. 午餐

大家一起来到水上公园,他们决定休息吃点东西。他们来到海滩边的野餐区,这里有桌子和遮荫树。在炎热的夏天的烈日下,珍妮享受着清凉的可口可乐和汉堡。铁蛋在赛百味买了火鸡胸三明治和番茄酱。他看到电视广告上说,赛百味的三明治是新鲜,健康,营养和低脂肪的。

史密斯太太在切一个巨大的西瓜并把切好的西瓜放在纸盘子上。

铁蛋:西瓜!那是我最喜欢的水果。
珍妮:你说什么?

Tiedan goes to America

铁蛋:西瓜。中文叫西瓜。我们还有黄瓤西瓜。

爱德华:黄瓤西瓜?我从来没见过。味道是一样的吗?

铁蛋:我想是一样的。它是很甜很好吃的。

35. 谈论中国

铁蛋：我不想让今天这么快结束……今天玩得真开心。谢谢你们带我来水上公园。

史密斯太太：这是我们的荣幸。我希望在中国旅游的时候，我们也能跟今天一样开心。

铁蛋：我要为你们计划每一分钟。我希望每天都能有趣而开心。我想让你们更加了解我的家乡和中国。

贝拉：我们可以买些草帽吗？我在电视上看到中国人会戴草帽？

铁蛋：你说的那些"草帽"现在并没有多少人戴了。只有在乡下或农村你才能看到有人戴。

36. 关于沙滩

泰德：嘿，珍妮，你为什么不和贝拉带铁蛋到海滩上玩。我肯定他会喜欢，可以用沙子搭一座城堡。

索菲亚：是的……，你就在那里，为什么不找一些贝壳。

铁蛋：贝壳？那是什么？

爱德华：贝壳…他们是生活在水里的生物的家。如果你把它放在耳朵旁边，你就可以听到大海的波浪声（将手放在耳朵边像握着一个贝壳）。

铁蛋：哦！我知道了。贝壳，在我的房间有一堆贝壳。我有时用它们做项链给我的朋友。

珍妮：自行车。你用自行车做项链吗？

铁蛋：不，贝壳。听起来像是自行车，但有一个E在结尾。

37. 学游泳 1

史密斯太太：好吧，今天的中文课就到这里。让我们走下海滩。我答应铁蛋今天我会教他游泳。每个人都带泳衣了吗？

所有人都来到海滩，穿上泳衣。铁蛋很想快点进入水中，跟史密斯太太上他的第一次游泳课。詹妮，爱德华，特德，索菲亚和贝拉已经在水里嬉戏，他们拍打水，飞溅的水珠洒在史密斯先生的身上。

铁蛋：嘿，这看起来很有趣。水是冷的？

史密斯太太：不。不是的。一旦你习惯了它，就不会这么想。最重要的是记住在这里游泳，水不深。如果你遇到了麻烦，你随时可以站起来。

铁蛋：好吧。站起来。

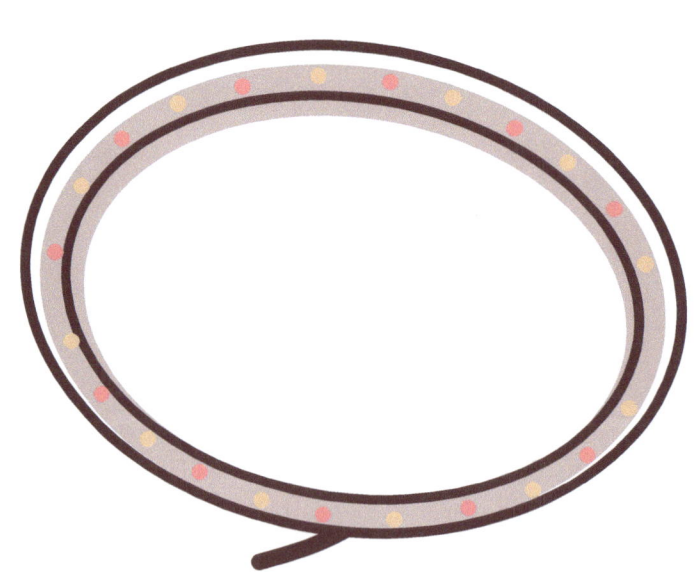

38. 学游泳 2

史密斯太太：首先，你必须有足够的勇气，把你的头和身体伸入水中。

铁蛋：把头伸入水……我知道了。

史密斯太太：下一步，在水下屏住呼吸。

铁蛋：屏住呼吸……我知道了。

史密斯太太：第三，放松一下，浮在水面。不要恐慌。如果你遇到麻烦，你随时可以站起来。

铁蛋：浮在水面……我知道了。

史密斯太太：第四，记住要慢慢呼吸。

铁蛋：慢慢呼吸……我知道了。

史密斯太太：第五，用你的手臂和脚划水。这样会帮助你漂浮。

铁蛋：用手脚划水……我知道了。

史密斯太太：最后的和最重要的……玩得开心！

铁蛋：玩得开心。我能做到！！

39. 在动物园

在美国,布朗克斯动物园是最大的城市动物园。它是在纽约的最北部。票价是成人30美元左右(13岁以上),儿童20美元(年龄2－13),老人25美元(65岁以上)。每月有一天捐款日,你可以为你心中的布朗克斯动物园支付票价。

铁蛋和珍妮星期六去布朗克斯动物园。当他们通过正门,听到了柔和的美洲音乐。他们参观了大象,老虎和各种猴子。他们记下了动物园喂养海狮的时间——通常是小孩子最开心的时间。在池塘里,他们还看到著名的粉红色

的火烈鸟。

他们停了一会儿来查看地图。然后他们向右边的道路走去，穿过小火车轨道他们看到了狮子，骆驼和长颈鹿。接下来，他们将参观亚洲野生动物广场。

40. 骑骆驼

工作人员说：在亚洲野生动物广场体验骑骆驼，会很有趣。

铁蛋说：我真的很想骑骆驼。

工作人员说：好吧，好吧，小男孩，请等一下。

好了，好了，小男孩，试着骑上去。

铁蛋发现一只鼻子穿绳的骆驼走到自己面前，跪下，好像在说：亲爱的主人，请坐上！铁蛋迅速跑上去，工作人员把他放到骆驼的驼峰中间。铁蛋坐好，员工拍了拍骆驼的脖子，它站了起来。

铁蛋说：嘿，骆驼比马高。骑在上面有点困难。

骆驼是温顺的。骆驼开始平静地走。铁蛋感觉很好。

他大声叫道:嘿!我骑上来了。没有什么是不可能的。嗯,这很有趣! 像中世纪的旅行者。

珍妮:嗯,铁蛋,摆个姿势,我来帮你拍张照。

41. 喂羊

在亲子乐园，珍妮支付了一美元买一些草。

铁蛋说：珍妮，这是什么？

珍妮说：这是山羊爱吃的干草和叶子。你可以买一些喂山羊。

铁蛋问：这好吃吗？

珍妮说：看看山羊。它们喜欢它。它们吃得真开心。

铁蛋：这对山羊是最好的食物，就像我们爱吃米饭一样。

42. 家庭聚会

铁蛋说：家庭聚会将在2:00开始，我都等不及了。我的新朋友瑞瑞会来，他正在路上。

珍妮说，太好了！我也邀请了我的所有好朋友。饮料也都准备好了。妈妈还烤了巧克力蛋糕。她做的蛋糕是世界上最好吃的。希望我们能玩得开心。

铁蛋说：当然了。我准备了我最好的衣服。你喜欢我用蓝色衬衫配牛仔裤吗？

珍妮：太完美了！

在2:30，门铃响了，珍妮打开门。

珍妮：我们都在这里了。请进来，瑞瑞。

Tiedan goes to America

珍妮：铁蛋，这是瑞瑞。大家静一下，他们来自中国。

珍妮：这些是我的朋友，布莱恩，弗莱德，汤姆。

铁蛋说：很高兴见到你们。我怎样才能记住你们所有人的名字？我最好做笔记。

珍妮：放心吧。我会给你我们的照片，然后，我在照片上写下他们的名字。

43. 参观美国小学

美国的学校就像一个公园。在学校前面有个大操场，后面有个大院子。操场上的草很柔软，很绿。铁蛋他们进入教室后，发现了一个巨大的卡片吊在天花板，上面写着，"我们班是第一棒的班级"。

墙上挂着许多活动时拍的照片。**铁蛋想：美国的学生是健康快乐的。每个人都在照相机前露出微笑。哦，他们的书包太轻了。**

教室里开辟了一个地方专门做手工。那里有许多蜡笔，彩色铅笔，剪刀，胶水和彩纸。学生的画都很有创意。

Tiedan goes to America

这是一节历史课。学生们围坐在老师周围。一个班级只有16个学生。他们在谈论第二次世界大战。

老师问大家：你认为谁应该对战争负责？

许多人回答，如，日本，德国，意大利等。

珍妮告诉铁蛋：在美国学校没有标准答案。你没必要遵循老师的意见，但是你必须给出能解释通的理由。

44. 暑假作业

在暑假期间不上课并不意味着孩子们停止学习。

珍妮有她的暑假作业——就是读100本书。她加入了家附近图书馆的阅读计划。珍妮和她的母亲列了一长串的阅读书目。因为她对昆虫很感兴趣，所以她借了很多有关昆虫方面的书。

为了更好的了解昆虫，珍妮开始饲养昆虫，观察它的生长发育并且写关于昆虫的日记。珍妮和铁蛋捉到一只蚂蚱，他们把它放在一个小玻璃瓶里，用塑料薄膜密封好，并在上面扎了许多洞。每一天，他们把一片树或蔬菜的叶子放在瓶子里。起初蚂蚱不肯吃,但几天之后,它就开始吃了。他们都非常高兴。

45. 铁蛋爸爸妈妈写给珍妮爸爸妈妈的邮件

亲爱的史密斯先生与夫人：

我们的儿子铁蛋，回来已经一个星期了。我们衷心感谢你们的热情款待。铁蛋给我们讲了许多关于他和你们在一起的事。他对人们之间友好相处印象深刻。他真的喜爱吃你做的意大利面条。他很幸运有这样一个美好的寄宿家庭。他每天给我们看他在美国照的照片。不仅他的英语大有进步，而且他更加了解美国的文化和生活。世界是平的，经济已经全球化发展。我希望他长大后能

Tiedan goes to America

在国外工作。这次寄宿经历真是硕果累累。他永远不会忘记这次美好的回忆。

再次从心底感谢你们。我们全家都在高兴地等待着明年你们全家会早点来拜访我们。

向全家问好。再见！

你的朋友吴，许

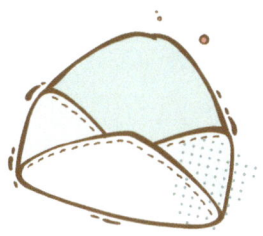

46. 珍妮妈妈写给铁蛋爸爸妈妈的邮件

亲爱的吴先生和许女士：

收到你们的邮件，我们又兴奋又感激。我们很高兴有这样一个可爱的男孩来我们这里做客。铁蛋开朗活泼。他做得非常好，他对纽约的生活很适应。铁蛋和珍妮在这里参观了很多地方，有学校，动物园和游乐园。他玩得很开心。

铁蛋的英语很好。开始我们与他交流有一点小问题，后来他能做一个演讲并回答问题，他帮我们全家赢了一次中国之行，让我们都非常高兴。他还教我们中文。铁蛋是我们了解中国的窗口。我们都期待着明年能去拜访你们。那么今天就先写到这儿。再见！

你们的朋友：爱丽丝

Preface

Don't wait until the third grade (8 years old) to start to learn the first foreign language, and don't wait until high school or college (16-18 years old) to start to learn a second language. It is just a waste of time and money. Simply take the time to immerse yourself in the adventures of Tiedan and his exciting travels within the United States. Follow in the footsteps of Tiedan and reward yourself with the benefits of learning a foreign language. In our youth is the promise of a golden future.

The book, Tiedan goes to America, illustrates Tiedan as a typical Chinese boy who has the good fortune of travelling to the US. Ordinary teaching materials or text in the standard form of simple and boring are avoided through dialogue scenes. The conversations in the book are commonly used, and simple beginners easily master the vocabulary. This set of textbooks can immensely raise children's interest in the United States as well as English and improve children's listening and speaking ability.

Similarly, the Chinese version allows children to

recognize multiple Chinese characters, basic dialogues, and spoken language expression. While we learn English, we can improve the Chinese language ability and master Chinese. The use of multi-lingual teaching method can master multiple languages on the condition that doesn't reduce the ability of any one language. Tiedan goes to America for you and your child as relaxed and happy to learn a foreign language.

Litao Xu

Tiedan goes to America

Recommendation

Tiedan goes to America is a very interesting book about the lodging experience of Tiedan in the United States making it an immersive read.

My first impression of Tiedan goes to America is that it is a true record of the challenges one might face traveling abroad. The story covers the preparation to leave for the United States, sending emails, taking a plane, passing through Customs, as well as the reluctance.Tiedan experiences leaving his host family before returning home. There is care in describing his embarrassment of having juice on his pants after carelessly knocking over his cup on the plane as well as his nervousness communicating with a salesman to buy drinks. He visits the school, plays in the park, goes shopping and to family gatherings. These are fictional experiences of Tiedan in the United States. What an exciting fantasy it is! The story is full of fun, in fact the phrase "Have fun!" is frequently used throughout the book. After Tiedan comes to the United States, he is warmly received by the boarding family. He gives them much joy with the gifts he brought with him from China .Tiedan is then so excited that he has trouble falling asleep on his first night in America. All of this, playing at the amusement

park, learning how to swim, riding a camel all combine to make Tiedan feel joyful. Luckily for Tiedan his good fortune goes beyond his travels to the US. While at the amusement park he gets interviewed, makes a speech and guesses a riddle, Tiedan wins the opportunity to invite the Smith family to China, making them feel delighted. Fourthly, it's mutual transmission of culture is essential in delivering the message of cross culture. During his lodgings in the United States, Tiedan came to know New York's nickname is the Big Apple, the United States was established in 1776, and the person on a dollar bill is the first president of the United States, George Washington. Tiedan also touched the etiquette culture when Americans have dinner, they will pray to God, the culinary culture about three meals a day, and the school culture that there is no standard answer in American school, that American students are encouraged to seek their own answers to problems and not rely heavily on the advice of teachers. Tiedan experience has taught him a great deal of the daily life of most American families.

    In the United States, Tiedan enjoyed the many splendid sceneries and attractive site-seeing locations, experienced the diversity of American culture from coast to coast as well as making some foreign friends.

WuXi Foreign Language School Dean Zhou

Tiedan goes to America

Main person

Tiedan — a Chinese boy
Jenny — an American girl
Mr. Wu — Tiedan's father
Mrs. Xu — Tiedan's mother
Ms. Qian — Tiedan's English teacher
RuiRui — Tiedan's new friend
Mr. Smith/ Jackson — Jenny's father
Mrs. Smith/ Alice — Jenny's mother
Ted — Jenny's elder brother
Edward — Jenny's younger brother
Sophia — Jenny's elder sister
Bella — Jenny's younger sister

Tiedan goes to America

1. Who is Tiedan

Tiedan is an energetic and friendly little boy. He is a 12 year old 6th grade student at an International Elementary school. He especially enjoys going to Happy Family Club (a multi-language multi-cultural Children's activity club). Tiedan can speak a little English, and is curious about everything. He likes to travel overseas and plans to go to America on a home stay program this summer. Let's join him.

2. Tiedan's diary

Date: Monday, June 22
Weather: Sunny

Summer is coming and it is becoming hotter. I hope to go to America soon. I want to learn English and study American culture. This is my preparation list before going to home stay:

① Collect the books and brochures about America

② Learn basic English

③ Apply for passport

④ Send an email to the home stay family

⑤ Make schedule: Plan how many days to stay, budget, destination, and purpose

⑥ Tell travel agency to book a flight and apply the visa

⑦ Exchange some money for dollars

⑧ Join overseas insurance

⑨ Prepare commonly used medicines

⑩ Buy gifts for home stay family

⑪ Pack up suitcase

My VISA hasn't been approved, and I have no idea of which travel agency to choose. I'd better ask Mom to help me.

Tiedan goes to America

3. An email from Tiedan to Jenny

Hi Jenny,

My name is Tiedan. I'm very happy to know you. I'm 12 years old, same as you. I have attached my picture to this email. My home is in the east part of Beijing. I'm a 6th grade elementary school student. At school I'm a Taekwondo club member. I like playing Asian chess and drawing, as well as Happy Family Club.

I live with my grandpa, grandma, my father and mother. Both my grandparents are over 70, but they are in good health. My father is an engineer at a software company, and my mother is a teacher. My uncle is also living in Beijing. He visits me almost every weekend. He is a professor at University. I'm eagerly awaiting for the summer to come. It will be lots of fun. I hope to meet you soon.

Yours Tiedan

4. Another email from Tiedan to Jenny

Hi Jenny,

Thank you very much for your email and pictures. I'm very happy to know you. Thank you very much for having me home stay with your family. This is the first time for me to go abroad. I am thrilled and excited.

I will arrive at New York Airport at 4 pm on July 8. Could your mom pick me up at the airport? I will fly by Air China CA982. I'm looking forward to meeting you.

Yours Tiedan

铁蛋去美国

Tiedan goes to America

5. At the airport

Tiedan goes to the check-in desk, shows the clerk his passport.

Tidan: I'd like to check in, please.

A clerk: Window seat or aisle seat?

Tidan: Aisle seat, thank you.

A clerk: This is the boarding pass. Please board at gate D before 11 o'clock.

Tidan: Thank you .

Tiedan goes around the airport. There are so many beautiful brand shops.

Tiedan: The goods are top quality. However the prices are so high that I can't afford it. I'd better leave here as soon as possible.

6. On the airplane

Annoucement: Please fasten your seatbelt and the plane will take off in ten minutes.

A flight attendant:What would you like to drink?

Tiedan: Apple juice, please.

A flight attendant:Would you like meat or fish?

Tiedan: Fish, please.

Tiedan thinks:Oh, so many foods! Bread with butter and fish and vegetable salad and sliced apple. Ah, they are very delicious.

Tiedan:Can I have another glass of apple juice?

A flight attendant answers, Yes, here you are.

Tiedan thinks: The drinks on an airplane are free to refill. Great!

Tiedan is so excited that he happens to knock over the cup.   The juice pours on his pants. He is embarrassed and nervous.

Tiedan: What can I do?

A flight attendant: It's alright, don't worry. I will clean it with a rag.

Tiedan:I appreciate your help.

A flight attendant: Don't mention it. It is my job.

7. America's history

Tiedan reads a book. It says, "America is a Federal Republic of 50 states. Washington is its' capital. The United Nation's Headquarters is in New York. Prior to Columbus discovering the land, the American Indian originally lived there. Later European immigrants moved in. A large number of people came to seek the American dream from all over Europe. In 1776, America won the War of Independence against the United Kingdom. The history of the United States began at that time."

Tiedan goes to America

 8. At immigration

An officer: May I see you passport, please?

Tiedan gives her his passport.

An officer: What's the purpose of your visit?

Tiedan:I'm here for a home stay program.

An officer: How long are you staying?

Tiedan:One month.

An officer: How much money do you have?

Tiedan :I have 500 dollars.

The office stamps Tiedan's passport. Tiedan passes the immigration desk.

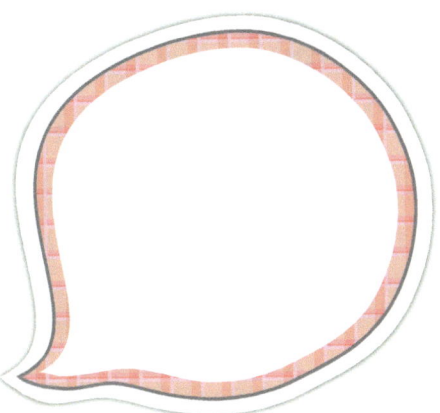

9. At customs

A customs officer: Do you have anything to declare?

Tiedan: No, I have nothing to declare.

A customs officer asks Tiedan to open his suitcase.

A customs officer: What's that?

Tiedan: This is for my personal use. These are gifts for my home stay family.

A customs officer lets Tiedan pack his suitcase and go.

Tiedan goes to America

10. At the airport

Tiedan thinks: What should I say first? Guess I should say "How do you do", cause this is our first time meeting each other. I have the cellphone number of Mrs. Smith. I will call her if I get confused. Oh! Look at all these Americans; they are all white skin, brown hair and blue eyes. They are carrying heavier luggage than me.

Tiedan sees his name is on the placard being held by someone. Tiedan goes nearer to see.

Mrs. Smith: Are you Tiedan? Glad to see you.

Tiedan: Excuse me, but could you speak more slowly?

Mrs. Smith: Oh, sorry. Are you Tiedan?

Tiedan: Yes! You must be Mrs Smith.

Mrs. Smith: Yes. Nice to meet you. You look just like your picture. We are happy to have you. Did you have a good flight?

Tiedan: The flight was smooth, but I am tired after a 14-hour flight. Anyway, I'm really happy to be here.

Mrs. Smith: You will be fine. Let's go now.

Tiedan goes to America

 11.Go home

Mrs. Smith and Tiedan get into a big car.

Mrs. Smith: Are you hungry, Tiedan?

Tiedan :Yes, a little. Thank you for picking me up, Mrs. Smith.

Mrs. Smith: Don't mention it. Call me Alice.

Tiedan : OK, Alice.

Tiedan thinks: So this is America. Everything is so big. Oh, look at that big American car. Aha, the cars are going on the right side of the street, same as in China.

Mrs. Smith: Do you know the other name of New York, Tiedan?

Tiedan: No, I don't.

Mrs. Smith:It is called The Big Apple. It's so attractive everyone wants to take a bite.

Tiedan: Yes, that's true.

Tiedan : There is McDonalds, and there is KFC. BigMacs are half price now. We have them in China, too.

12. At home

Mrs. Smith: We've arrived! Tiedan get out and come inside.

Tiedan: What a big house! There is a garden behind.

Mrs. Smith: Tiedan, this summer, this is your home.

Tiedan: Is that so? Splendid! I can't believe it.

Jenny: Welcome to our family. I'll show you around. There are 4 bed rooms upstairs. Kitchen, Dining room and living room are downstairs. This is your room.

Tiedan: Oh, it's pretty! There is a yellow closet, a red cabinet, a yellow desk, a pink bookshelf, and a blue bed. There are many books and two robots on the bookshelf. I can see the flowers and trees from the window. Is the room all for me?

Jenny: Yes, it is. The cabinet below is yours. You can hang your jacket in this closet and put your other clothes in this cabinet. Please put laundry in the basket. We usually do the laundry twice a week. If you want to clean your room, please use the vacuum cleaner.

Tiedan: (Suddenly) Jenny, where is the toilet?

Jenny : You mean the bathroom? Come with me, this is the bathroom.

Tiedan goes to America

 # 13.Dinner time1--manners

Tiedan: What time do you usually have dinner?

Mrs. Smith: We eat around seven o'clock. It will be ready soon. Tiedan hurry and wash your hands for dinner.

Mrs. Smith: Tiedan, please sit between Jackson and Ted.

Mr. Smith: Come on, Tiedan. You are sitting next to me.

Tiedan: OK.

After praying, they start to eat. Tiedan sees there are many plates of food on a long table. One big plate of chicken is in the middle. Before Tiedan, there is one plate, a knife and a spoon and a fork. Though there are no chopsticks, Tiedan is not confused. Tiedan takes the knife in his right hand and the fork in the left. That's the manner for western food. Tiedan also knows he can't speak with his mouth full of food.

Tiedan goes to America

 14. Dinner time2—foods

Mrs. Smith takes one bowl of salad and some fruits, then passes it to Ted.

Mrs. Smith: We always take foods in turn like this. Take as much as you would like, Tiedan.

Tiedan: Yes, thank you.

Mrs. Smith: Is there anything you don't like to eat?

Tiedan: No, I like American food very well.

Mrs. Smith: Want to try some of this meat, Sophia?

Sophia: No thanks. I am on a diet now.

Mr. Smith: How do you like it, Tiedan?

Tiedan: Oh, yes. It's really delicious!

Mr. Smith: Eat as much as you like.

Tiedan: No more please. I'm full.

Mrs. Smith: What do you usually eat for supper at home?

Tiedan: We usually eat fish or meat with veggies, rice or steamed bun and porridge. That's a typical Chinese meal.

Mrs. Smith nodded: Uh-huh.

15. Presents

After dinner, as everyone is here,

Tiedan stands up and speaks loudly:

Everybody, presents from China for you.

Jackson, this is for you. It is a picture I painted.

Mr. Smith: Great! Let's see. I'll put it here on the refrigerator?

Tiedan: That's nice.

Tiedan: Here this is for you, Jenny.

Jenny: Can I open it?

Ah! It is a T-shirt like the one you're wearing.

Tiedan: Yes, it is. Mom bought me a new T-shirt. I like it very much, so I bought the same as a present to you. Do you like it?

Jenny: Oh, yes! Thank you for the lovely gift, Tiedan.

Tiedan: You're welcome. I am very glad that you like it.

Mrs. Smith: OK, everyone, it's getting late. Everyone get to bed.

Everyone: OK, Mom. Thank you, Tiedan!

Tiedan goes to America

16. Good night

Tiedan washes his face and brushes his teeth. He goes to bed, but he is so excited that he can hardly get to sleep.

Tiedan thinks:This bed is so soft and comfortable. The night is quiet and long. Even though I completely forgot to say "how do you do", they could understand my English. Sometimes I heard the exact phrase I learned in the story. It was amazing. I could not understand what they said exactly, but I could guess pretty close. I dropped some corn on the floor, but Mrs. Smith was not angry. They are so kind to me.

"Good for me! Good for me! It is the first step that is troublesome. I'm gonna be OK. Practice makes perfect. I will speak more and more."

17. Morning

Early one morning in the blazing heat of summer, on the tree a cicada is singing a song. Tiedan is awakened by his foreign friend Jenny.

Jenny: Wake up sleepy head, time to rise and shine... Greet the day with a smile.

Tiedan: (sleepily)... Leave me alone, I'm sleepy.

Jenny: Come on, Tiedan! Don't waste the day, you'd better get up.

Tiedan: Uggg !! Are you always so cheerful in the morning? By the way, what time is it?

Jenny: (Jumping on the bed) Come on !!! get up ! It's already 7 am. We're going to have a great day.

Tiedan: (A little more awake) Really, what's so special about today?

Jenny:(Standing at the door) Well, get dressed and come downstairs and you'll find out!

Tiedan quickly puts on his pants and T-shirt and a pair of socks. After washing his face, he goes down the steps.

18. Breakfast

Mrs. Smith: We usually have cereal for breakfast. I think perhaps you don't like cereal. Could you eat some French toast for breakfast?

Tiedan: Great!

When Tiedan sees French toast, he is a little surprised.

Tiedan: I thought it was French bread. How did you make it?

Mrs. Smith: It's easy. You cut the bread into pieces. Then you add one egg into milk and mix it. Next cover both sides of the bread with the liquid. Heat oil or butter in a frying pan. Put the bread in and fry this side. After 2 or 3 seconds, turn over and fry the other side. At last, the French toast is done. You can put maple syrup on it.

Tiedan: OK!

Tiedan goes to America

 **19. Talking about Amusement park**

After breakfast, everyone is ready to go.

Tiedan to Mr. Smith: Jackson, What's going on, everyone is so excited!

Mr. Smith: As they should be Tiedan. Today we are all going to the amusement center and water park.

Tiedan: Hmmmm... What's an amusement park?

Sophia: Have you ever heard of a place called "Disney Land" or a famous mouse called "Mickey"?

Tiedan: Of course. Everyone has heard of Mickey Mouse. I like their movies and animations, too.

Sophia: Well, if you know Disney Land, the amusement park is just like that. Maybe a little smaller though. The water park is like a day at the beach.

Tiedan: WOW!!! It sure sounds like a lot of fun. Have you been there before?

Sophia: Yea, many times. It's one of our favorite places to go on these hot days.

20. Talking about swim

Ted: Hey Tiedan, have you ever been surfing?

Tiedan: I have surfed the internet, is that what you mean?

Ted: (Full of laughter) No, I mean, surf on the waves (makes hand motions of water).

Tiedan: Oh surf on the water. No, I'm not too good a swimmer.

Ted: Hmm, we'll need to get you some quick lessons on swimming. You'd better go talk to mom about swimming. She's the best one in the family.

Tiedan: HEY! Mom, can you teach me how to swim before we get to the water park?

Mrs. Smith: Swimming is a wonderful sports; however it is not easy for a beginner. First, you have to be brave enough to put your head even your body into the water. Next hold your breath under the water. Third, relax and try to float on the surface of water. Forth, learn to breathe in the water. After all, I can tell you all about swimming, but the real learning takes place at the water. I'll help you when we get there.

Tiedan: (Thinks to himself) I hope I can learn how to swim, my friends back in China will be so happy for me.

21. On the way

Everyone gets into the car and heads toward the park. Along the way everyone is sitting down enjoying the scenery. All of a sudden Edward starts to sing his favorite song. "Old McDonald had a farm" Tiedan is happy to sing along as this is one of the songs he learned at his Happy Family Club meetings.

Tiedan: I know this song, it's about a man who owns a farm and on this farm there are many animals. We say the name of the animal and the sound it makes, right?

Edward: That's right Tiedan. You can start us off.

All together they begin the verse: Old McDonald had a farm... E, I, E, I, O, and on this farm he had a duck, E, I, E, I, O. with a "quack quack" here and a "quack quack" there, everywhere a "quack quack" E, I E, I, O.

Edward: WOW!! Tiedan, you did great. You even made the right sound.

Tiedan: Thanks Edward. That is one of the songs I learned in our Happy Family Club. I think we sang it nearly every time we met.

Tiedan goes to America

22. Talking about school

Tiedan: I also know a song called, "Wheels on the bus", do you know that one?

Bella: I do! That's one of my favorites. When I go to school we always sing that song.

Tiedan: I've never ridden on a school bus before. I saw a picture of an American school bus once. It was yellow and big. It is stronger than any other cars.

Bella: How do you get to school Tiedan? Do you have to walk there or does your dad drive you?

Tiedan: Well, our home is close to the school, so I usually walk there with my mom. Sometimes my dad drives me.

Bella: What is your favorite subject?

Tiedan: English is my favorite subject. Mr. Qian is my English teacher. She speaks English very fluently and tells us many English stories. We all like her stories.

Bella: That's great.

23. Arrived

Mr. Smith: Okay everyone, we're here at the park. Now some basic rules:

1. PUT your trash in a can

2. NEVER go anywhere ALONE

3. If you get lost... go to the front gate and stay there. Either your mom or I will be there

4. The most important rule is... EVERYONE HAS A GREAT TIME

Everyone gets out of the car and starts heading towards the gate.

Tiedan: This is really going to be a lot of fun!! I'm so excited.

Mrs. Smith: Tiedan, you stay with one of your brothers or sisters. This is a big place and you can easily get lost. So, always know where they are. Okay?

Tiedan: Yes, I'll be careful.

Jenny: Tiedan, stay with me and we'll have all the fun. I know all the best rides and best food to eat.

Tiedan: Okay, sounds like I am in for a treat.

24. Wait in line

Everyone enters the park and begins to have a wonderful time. Jenny and Tiedan head off to the rides. They are standing in a long line waiting to get on the Roller Coaster.

Jenny: This is the biggest roller coaster at the park; it's called "The Beast". It's made entirely of wood and has 3 big hills and some great curves. Have you ever been on a roller coaster before?

Tiedan: No, not this big ! We have a small park back in Beijing that has a small roller coaster. The park also has a Ferris wheel and a Pirate boat and a Merry-go-round.

Jenny: Really! I like a ferris wheel. You can see the whole park from there.

Tiedan: This line is not moving very fast... How long will it takes us to get to the front?

Jenny: I don't know, but it is well worth the wait. I hope you don't get scared easily.

Tiedan: No way!! The scarier it is the more I like it.

25. Ride on roller coaster

The two wait in line a little while longer and eventually make it to the front of the line. Jenny decides that they will sit at the front of the train.

Jenny: These are the best seats Tiedan! Come on and sit down and put on your safety belt.

Tiedan: WOW! It sure is a big ride. Why do they call it the Beast?

Jenny: You will find out! Just don't get scared.

Tiedan: Okay... LET'S GO!!

The two rocket over the hills and down the twist and turns. Both are screaming with laughter and excitement. Tiedan is having a great time and can't wait to take another ride.

铁蛋去美国

 26. Fun house

After the ride on the coaster, Jenny and Tiedan decide to head over to the Fun House.

Tiedan: Where are we going now Jenny?

Jenny: It's called the Fun House. Inside are some mirrors that make you look silly. Some will make you look taller or shorter or fatter or even thinner.

Tiedan: Oh, we have something like that back in China to. In Chinese we call it "HahaJing".

Jenny:Sounds like the people in China have a lot of fun things to do.

Tiedan: Sure, we have lots of fun things to do. My favorite is watching the fireworks.

Jenny: Fireworks!! I love watching fireworks; we go to the park on July 4th and see them.

Tiedan:In China, you can see fireworks almost every day. Maybe a birthday or a holiday or just any reason at all.

Jenny and Tiedan enter the Fun House and we can hear all the laughter and happiness from the people inside. Later they emerge with smiles from ear to ear.

27. Take a break

Jenny: Hey look over there, its mom and dad! I think them went to the shops to buy some souvenirs.

Tiedan: Oh great! I'm thirsty. I sure could use a drink.

Jenny: MOM——DAD!! (SHOUTS to Mr. and Mrs. Smith)

Tiedan: They heard you. They are coming this way.

Jenny and Tiedan meet Mr. and Mrs. Smith in the park center just beside the water fountain. Tiedan is thirsty and ask Mr. Smith for a drink.

Tiedan: Mr. Smith... Ohm... I mean Jackson. Can I get something to drink please?

Mr. Smith: Sure Tiedan, what would you like?

Tiedan: I've always wanted to try that drink with lemon. I saw it once on a TV show for 5 cents.

Mr. Smith: Oh. You want to try some lemonade. I think it will cost more than 5 cents though. Let's go over to the concession stand and check it out.

Tiedan goes to America

28. Buy drinks 1

Mr. Smith and Tiedan head over to the concession stand while Mrs. Smith and Jenny stand near the water fountain taking a break.

Inside the concession stand are lots of thirsty people. Everyone stands in a long line and waits their turn at the counter. Tiedan sees lots of items to choose from on the menu, such as tea, juice, milk, and sodas, eventually spotting the Lemonade.

Tiedan: WOW! A large cup of lemonade is $ 5.00. That's really expensive.

Mr. Smith: Yes, it is. I think it would be good for you to order the drink.

Tiedan: What? I'll be nervous talking to someone I don't know.

Mr. Smith: I'm sure you can do it. Just keep it simple and speak slowly.

Tiedan: Okay, I'll try! Here it goes.

29. Buy drinks 2

Tiedan walks up to the counter and with a hard swallow he opens his mouth to speak. The cashier behind the counter looks at Tiedan and with great patience listens to him.

Tiedan: Excuse me; I would like a drink please.

Cashier: Okay, what drink would you like?

Tiedan: I want the medium lemonade with ice.

Cashier: Do you want fresh lemon in it?

Tiedan: What? What does "fresh" mean?

Cashier: "fresh" means... not old.

Tiedan: Uhhhh... Okay, I want some fresh lemon in the drink.

Cashier: Your drink is $3.50.

Tiedan: Okay, here is a $5 dollar bill. Do I get some change?

Cashier: Yes, of course... your change is $1.50.

Tiedan: Thank you very much.

Cashier: Have a nice day at the park.

Tiedan goes to America

30. Interview

Tiedan and Mr. Smith go back to where Jenny and Mrs. Smith are waiting by the water fountain. An ABC reporter with a photographer comes to Tiedan.

Reporter: Hi, we are making a TV program of travel. May I interview you?

Tiedan: Yes, of course. I am an exchange student from China.

Reporter: Great! Can you share some opinions of Americans with our audience while we take a video?

Tiedan: OK. Let me try.

Reporter: I will ask you a simple quiz later. If you are correct, you will win a round trip to China for your home stay family.

Tiedan goes to America

31. Speech

The reporter: It is a wonderful day today, and now I'm reporting from the amusement park. We have Tiedan, an elementary student from China. He is wearing a blue cotton T-shirt. Now, Tiedan, please share some of your impressions of America with our audience.

Tiedan: It is the first time for me to come to New York. It's all been wonderful. I am very happy that everyone I meet and talk to is very friendly. I have been able to make lots of new friends.

Today I came to this amusement park. I rode a roller coaster called The Beast. It was crazy. I will try some more things. I am sure I will have a good time here. In the next few days, I will visit Museums, a zoo, an aquarium, and also an American school. It is a great experience for me.

Thank you everyone!

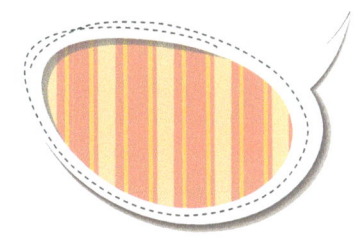

32. Quizes

The reporter: You gave a nice speech. Next, let me give you the quiz. That's a challenge. Are you ready?

Tiedan: Yes, I am.

The reporter: 1.What's the nickname of New York?

Tiedan: Big Apple .(thinking of what Mrs. Smith told him on the way home)

The reporter:You are smart. Correct. Next, when was America established?

Tiedan: In 1776. (thinking of the book he read on the airplane)

The reporter: The third question is: Who's face is on the one dollar bill?

Tiedan: George Washington, the first president.(thinking of the other day Jenny told him)

The reporter: It's terrific. You are all correct. You won the round trip. Congratulations!

Tiedan: I'm so lucky. Thank you!

 33. Happy news

Mr. Smith: WOW!! That is amazing. When do we leave?

The reporter: That is the great part. You can choose any time in the next year to go. ALL of YOU!!

Tiedan: WOW!! That means that you can come to China and visit my family and see some of the great places I've been telling you about.

Jenny: Yes. Isn't it GREAT NEWS, I can't wait to tell the others.

The whole family goes off in search of Edward and Bella and Sophia and Ted eager to tell them the good news. Finally, they found them. Jenny is first to tell the others the good news and they all rejoice at the prospect of going to China.

Tiedan goes to America

34. Lunch

With all the family together in the water park, they decide it's a good time to take a break and get something to eat. They head over to the beach area where there are some picnic tables and shade trees. As they sit under the hot summer sun Jenny enjoys a cool refreshing Coca Cola and Cheeseburger. Tiedan buys a Turkey Breast Sandwich with ketchup from Subway. He saw it on a TV ad. It said the Subway's sandwiches are fresh, healthy, nutritious, and low-fat. Mrs. Smith is carving a huge watermelon and laying out the pieces on paper plates.

Tiedan: Xigua ! That's my favorite fruit.

Jenny: What did you say?

Tiedan: Xigua. It's Chinese for Watermelon. We have a watermelon that is YELLOW on the inside.

Edward: A yellow watermelon? I've never seen a yellow one before. Does it taste the same?

Tiedan: I think so. It's sweet and delicious.

35. Talking about China

Tiedan: I never want this day to end. I'm having such a great time. Thank you for taking me to the water park today.

Mrs. Smith: It was our pleasure. I hope we have just as much fun in China as we are having here today.

Tiedan: I will plan every minute of your visit. I hope everyday can be fun and interesting. I want you to learn a lot about my hometown and about China.

Bella: Can we all get those straw hats that I see the Chinese wearing on TV?

Tiedan: We call those "Caimao" and not many people wear those anymore. You might see them out in the country side on a farm.

36. At the beach

Ted: Hey Jenny, why don't you and Bella take Tiedan down to the beach. I'm sure he'd love to play in the sand and make a sand castle.

Sophia: Yeah and while you're at it, why not look for some shells.

Tiedan: Shells? What is that?

Edward: Shells, they are the home to some of the animals that live in the water. If you put your ear up to it, you can hear the ocean waves. (Puts hands up to ear as if holding a shell)

Tiedan: Oh! I know. Beike, I have a bunch of them in my room. I sometimes make a necklace with them for my friend.

Jenny: Bike..you make a necklace with a bike?

Tiedan: No. Beike. Sounds like B I K E, but with an E sound at the end.

37. Learn to swim 1

Mrs. Smith: Okay everyone, that's enough Chinese lessons for today. Let's head down to the beach. I promised Tiedan I would show him how to swim today. Did everyone bring their swim suit?

Everyone heads down to the beach and into their swim suits. Tiedan is eager to get into the water and take his first swimming lesson. Jenny, Edward, Ted, Sophia and Bella are already jumping around in the water and splashing Mr. Smith with buckets of water.

Tiedan: Hey, what fun! Is the water cold?

Mrs. Smith: No, not really. Once you get used to it. The most important thing to remember about swimming here is that the water is NOT very deep and you can easily just stand up if you get into any trouble.

Tiedan: Okay. Stand up.

38. Learn to swim 2

Mrs. Smith:First, you have to be brave enough to put your head even your body into the water.

Tiedan: Head into water... GOT IT.

Mrs. Smith:Next hold your breath under the water.

Tiedan: Hold breath... GOT IT.

Mrs. Smith:Third, relax and try to float on the surface of water. Don't panic if you get into trouble. You can stand up anytime.

Tiedan: Float... GOT IT.

Mrs. Smith:Forth, remember to breathe slowly.

Tiedan:breathe slow... GOT IT.

Mrs. Smith:Fifth, keep moving your arms and feet. It will help you float.

Tiedan:Keep moving... GOT IT.

Mrs. Smith:Last thing and the most important⋯ HAVE FUN!

Tiedan:HAVE FUN. I can do that!!

39. At the Zoo

The largest metropolitan zoo in the U.S. is the Bronx Zoo. It is in the northern part of New York City. The ticket is about $30 for an adult(Age 13+), $20 for a child(Age 2-13), $25 for a senior (Age 65+). There is a donation day every month. You can pay the price of how you value the zoo.

Tiedan and Jenny go to the Bronx Zoo on Saturday. As they enter through the main gate, they listen to gentle African music. They visit elephants, tigers and monkeys of all kinds. They check the zoo information for feeding times for the Sea lions, always a fun time for the kids. At the pond, they see the famous Pink Flamingos.

They pause for a moment to check their map. Then they head to the right and over the train tracks to see the lions, camels, and giraffes.

Next, they will visit Wild Asia Plaza.

Tiedan goes to America

40. Ride a camel

A staff: Ride a camel around Wild Asia Plaza. That will be lots of fun.

Tiedan: I really want to ride a camel.

A staff: Okay, all right, little boy, just a second.

OK, ready now, little boy, try to get on.

Tiedan found a camel wearing the rope coming near. The camel immediately knelt down, as if to say: "dear guests please get on!" Tiedan quickly rushed out, the staff took him to the middle of the camel's hump. Tiedan was seated, the staff pated camel's neck, he stood up.

Tiedan: Hey, the camel is higher than a horse. It is a bit difficult to get on.

The camel is docile. The camel starts to walk calmly. Tiedan feels very well.

He shouts: Wee! I got on. Nothing is impossible. Well, this is so fun! Like a traveler in the Middle Ages.

Jenny: Well, Tiedan, pose, I'll take a picture of you.

41. Feed goats

At the Parent-child paradise, Jenny pays a dollar to get some grass.

Tiedan: Jenny, what is this?

Jenny: That is the goat's dry grass and leaves. You can buy some to feed the goats.

Tiedan: Is it good to eat?

Jenny: Look at the goats. They love it. They are enjoying it very much.

Tiedan: It is the best food for goats, as rice is for us.

Tiedan goes to America

42. Homeparty

Tiedan: The home party will begin at 2:00. I can hardly wait. My new friend RuiRui will come to the party, he's coming now.

Jenny: Great! I have invited all my friends, too. All the drinks are set. Mom has baked chocolate cakes. Her cakes are the best in the world. Hope you've enjoyed yourself.

Tiedan: Sure. I've laid out your best clothes. How do you like my blue shirt with jeans?

Jenny: Oh, perfect!

At 2:30, the doorbell rings. Jenny opens the door.

Jenny: We're all here. Come in, RuiRui.

Jenny: Tiedan, your friend RuiRui is here. Everyone, they both are from China.

Jenny: These are my friends, Bryan, Fred, and Tom.

Tiedan: Nice to meet you. How can I ever remember all your names? I'd better take notes.

Jenny: Take it easy. I will show you our pictures later. I will write down their names on the picture.

43. Visit American school

American schools are like a park. They have large play grounds in the front and big backyards. The grass on the playground is quite soft and green. When they enter the classroom, they find a big card is hanging from the ceiling, it says, "We are the NO.1 class".

On the wall, there are many pictures taken of activities.

Tiedan:(thinks) They are happy and healthy. Everyone smiles before the camera. Oh, their school bags are so light.

There is a craft corner in the back. There are many crayons, color pencils, scissors, glue, and color paper. The drawings are very creative.

It is a history class. The students are sitting around a teacher. There are only 16 students in one class. They are talking about the Second World War.

Teacher asks: Who do you think should be responsible for the war?

Many sorts of answers come out, such as, Japan, Germany, Italy and so on.

Jenny tells Tiedan: There are no standard answers in American school. It is not necessary to follow the teacher's opinion. However you have to give your soundful reason.

44. Summer Homework

During summer vacation just because school is out doesn't mean that kids stop learning.

Jenny has her summer homework—to read 100 books. She joins the reading program of the library nearby. Jenny and her mother made a long list of reading materials. Because she is interested in insects, she borrowed many books on it.

In order to know much about insects, Jenny starts to feed insects and inspects its growth and writes a diary about them. Jenny and Tiedan catch a locust. They put it in a small glass Jar, and seal the cover with plastic. They make many holes on the top. Every day, they put a leaf of a tree or vegetable in the bottle. At first the locust doesn't eat, but after a few days it begins to eat. They are very happy with it.

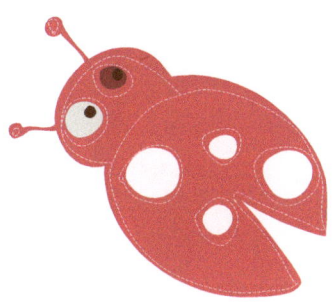

45. An email From Tiedan's parents

Dear Mr. and Mrs. Smith,

　　It has been already a week since our son Tiedan came back. We would like to express our hearty appreciation to you for your warm and kind hospitality to our son. He was surprised by the friendliness of people, and he really loved the pasta you made. He was so lucky to have such a wonderful host family. He shows us his album every day. It is not only his English that has improved, but he knows the culture and life in America. Economy is global and the world is flat. This home stay experience was really fruitful for him. He will never forget his beautiful memories as long as he lives. We would like to thank you again from the bottom of our hearts. We are looking forward to your family early visit to us next year.

　　Best Regards to your family.

Yours friend,
Wu and Xu

46. An email to Tiedan's father and mother

Dear Mr. Wu and Ms. Xu,

I am very excited and grateful to receive your email. We were so happy to have such a wonderful boy like Tiedan in our home. Tiedan is Cheerful and lively. He did very well and enjoyed his stay in New York. He and Jenny did a lot of visits to schools, a zoo, and an amusement park. He had a lot of fun.

Tiedan's English is pretty good. We had a little trouble understanding him at first. Later, he was able to make a speech and answer the quiz. He won a round trip to China for us. We were so happy. He also taught us a little Chinese. Tiedan is a gateway for us to learn about China. We are all looking forward to visiting you next year. Well, I must close for now.

Your friend,
Alice

www.ingramcontent.com/pod-product-compliance
Lightning Source LLC
Chambersburg PA
CBHW041516220426
43668CB00003B/39